THE MAYOR HAS A HAMMER

JIM SCHUTZ

THE MAYOR HAS A HAMMER
Finalist, Blue Light Book Award 2025

Copyright ©2025 by Jim Schutz

All rights reserved. Printed in the United States of America. No part of this book may be used or reproduced in any manner whatsoever without written permission except in the case of brief quotations embodied in critical articles and reviews. For information contact:

BLUE LIGHT PRESS
www.bluelightpress.com
Email: bluelightpress@aol.com

1ST WORLD LIBRARY
PO Box 2211
Fairfield, Iowa 52556
www.1stworldpublishing.com

BOOK & COVER DESIGN
Griffith Ballard, Lindsley Ballard, Jim Schutz
jim@localgovernmentpoetry.com
griffithballarddesigns@gmail.com

AUTHOR PHOTO
Michael Ashley
michael@lifeisnotstill.com

FIRST EDITION

ISBN: 978-1-4218-3579-2

Library of Congress Cataloging-in-Publication Data

For the local government professionals who dedicate their lives to building community and caring for the commons

Preface

The people who work in local government are my heroes. All of them. Ask them why they got into local government, and they most often talk about helping people and improving communities. They are capable and innovative and do thousands of things that improve people's lives, often without fanfare, recognition, or even awareness. They deserve to be celebrated in the most profound way — which is why I turned to poetry.

Since almost 20 of my over 30 years in local government were as an assistant city manager or city manager, readers will see their communities through those eyes — sometimes adoring, sometimes jaded. I have enormous respect for government employees, elected officials, and community members, and I hope, in return, they will give me the leeway to poke a bit at some of our daily trials and struggles. In a way, these are all love poems, but I sometimes show my love in unconventional ways.

My wish is that city managers, and all public officials, see themselves somewhere in this poetry collection. Here, I bow down and sing your praises. You are the uncommon ones who make the commons work for everyone.

Table of Contents

Part 1: For the Love of Public Service

Confessions of an Accomplishoholic 3
The Giver 5
Tragedy of the Commoners 7
City Hall 8
City Council Chambers 10
Pride of Lions 11
Swearing In 13
Ribbon Cutting 14
Grandmayor 15
Pronouns 17
My Favorite Resident 18
Song to My Local Government People 19

Part 2: Colleagues: Can't Work With 'Em, Can't Work Without 'Em

A Conversation Between the Library and
  Recreation Departments on the Eve of Their Merger 23
The Government Zoo 25
Intern Wanted 27
The Great Professor 29
Labor of Love 31
The Mountain 32
Haiku for Retiring City Planner Bob Brown 34
Department Director Annual Retreat 35
Partners 38

Part 3: Getting Through the Day

Putting on My Thick Skin 43
City Manager Gulliver 45
Version Control 46
Informal Authority 47
Like Talking to a Tree 48
Run the City Like a Business 49
Little Free Library 50
Truth or Dare, Frigidaire? 51
Covert Maneuvers at Safeway 52
White Vests 54
Punch Drunk 56

Part 4: Dreaming On

The Mayor Has a Hammer 59
Open Time for Public Comment 61
Quietly Listening to Public Comment at the
   City Council Meeting 62
The Municipal Performance Evaluation as a Love Sonnet 63
Tilting at Windmills 64
Municipal Drinking Games 65
A.H. (After Humans) 66
Hollow Man 68
Not Your Turn to Speak 69
Don't Run for City Council 71
Candidates 73
Help Wanted: City Manager (Applicants Apply Within) 74
Notes 75

Part 1

For the Love of Public Service

Confessions of an Accomplishoholic

The other newborns wrapped in their pink and blue tortillas
lay around me screeching,
as if they didn't have nine months to prepare
for this eventuality.

Me, already making my list:
eat, get vaccines, check the car seat they'll put me in.
Is it customary to tip the nursing staff?
I'm as yet a little light on cash.

Each decade goes by defined by my endless lists,
including my years as city manager:
House everyone, pave the roads, build parks,
make sure fires get put out, criminals get caught.

It becomes clear I am an addict,
seeking that elusive sense of achievement,
an unholy desire to move at full throttle —
get shit done.

To stop the madness, I try fly fishing in Alaska.
My wizened guide silently observes
as I haul in my fifth trout, then he winks at me and says,
"You really hog-tie them fish!"

"Slow down," he instructs, "one should *play* the fish,
get to know its personality — is it a fighter, a lover?"
He goes on: "When you let it go, does it sulk off
or flash its sequined skin with a flourish?"

"You," he says, poking my beige vest, "tie it up.
You beat it with a hose, muscle it in,
drag it to shore." I look down
at the trout in my guilty hands.

It looks up at me, panting, eyes bulging.
My fly hook pokes through its upper lip,
bobbing like a cigar, as it says to me:
"What the hell, dude?"

The Giver

I hear you're happy in your job,
content and untroubled,
but my public works director position is open,
and I can give it to you.

I can give you a budget five times beyond your current.
I can give you a legion of loyal employees,
enough machinery to move mountains.
I'm not just wooing — I'm begging,
casting my spells to turn a *no* into a *yes*.
It's what I do.

I drive across the bay to plead my case,
arriving at your doorstep — uninvited,
with a six-pack of Belgian ale, your favorite,
a novel about the romance of public service,
and my irresistible 11-year-old daughter,
who can melt resolve with the faintest of smiles.

I can give you the job of a lifetime.
You've been mucking about in the minors,
but I can boost you to the big leagues.

Yes, I can give you more money, and a car too,
and your own shiny new castle on the bay
to rule as you see fit.

I can drape you in capital projects,
and all the funding to do them.
I can give you everything you've ever wanted,
in this shining city of excellence.

And when you took the job
and died five months later of a heart attack,
I can't help but wonder, each endless night,
if I gave that to you too.

Tragedy of the Commoners

> *"Tragedy of the Commons" is when individual
> self-interest depletes a shared resource, harming all.*

They're nothing but bloated bureaucrats,
proclaims the real estate king,
a bit of bile erupting in his mouth.
He then asks me what city staffers want most.
To help their communities flourish, I proclaim,
to improve their own wisp of the world.

Nonsense, he mocks me, it's to get their pension.
His confidence absolute, unburdened
by any chromosomes of compassion.

To him, I am a commoner, living off his taxes,
driving my 12-year-old Ford Fusion
to night meetings at City Hall,
fundraisers at the public school.
A rube that will never know Aruba.
A boor never to see Bora Bora.

A life of service belittled
by the self-absorbed world.
If a commoner, then the rarest form.
The uncommon ones
who make the commons work
for everyone.

City Hall

There's nothing more that I adore
than the doors to City Hall.
The doors that open conversation, open debate,
open empathy, open hearts.

As if shrouded — the place you never think of,
or only to pay a ticket or wait in line for a license.
But City Hall is where the magic happens.

The wizard behind the curtain — when you
drive the city's streets, use its crosswalks,
launch your dream business, stroll your dog to a park,
flush the toilet, turn on a faucet,
need a police officer or paramedic.

Start on the front steps of City Hall.
Is it confident and stately, or unassuming and scrappy?

Wander inside to inspect its lungs and arteries, its nerves.
Go silent and hear the quiet breathing of the building,
how blood pumps through drywall and ceramic tile.

The hallways exhaling the same feeling as the Louvre —
wondrous delights await those who seek.
Except in this case, Mona is down the hall
in the city clerk's office,
and Lisa is upstairs at the planning and zoning counter.

A building full of people called to service,
to balance wildly competing opinions and agendas,
simply trying to make the city a better place
than how they found it.

If only City Hall were seen as it truly is —
its doors leading directly into the future
of your city, of all cities,
into the sublime notion of hometown.

City Council Chambers

I stand alone
in the city council chambers,
slow motion twirling, taking it all in.

Now as innocent as the spring's first trillium,
it will soon host an epic cage match
lasting until every punch has been thrown,
every folding chair hurled.

I stand alone
under the dank glow of fluorescent lights,
feeling the false calmness
like the steady retreat of the ocean as it fades
to greet the tsunami.

On their masts, the US, California, and city flags
cast their eyes downward in the stillness.
Soon they'll be crackling with wind from the podium,
and may be torn to whistling shreds
before the final gavel strikes.

Now, I stand alone,
I breathe in its thin carpeting, its worn chairs,
this humble chamber of democracy.
And it is beautiful.

Pride of Lions

The day I was entrusted to care for the three lions,
there was a formal ceremony.
I remember raising my right hand,
taking an oath.

Was it more like a wedding, a celebration
that I was conjoined to the three lions,
or was it more like one fine, final meal,
before I was shoved into the Colosseum arena,
facing either glory or gore?

The first lion — *City Council*.
It seemed affectionate with its chuffing and purring,
at least enough to choose me as city manager,
the three lions' caretaker.
But the lion who giveth may also taketh away.
I knew that well, watching so many other caretakers
disemboweled or devoured.
This one, though, did seem friendly enough,
letting me bring it meals and comb its mane.

The second lion — *City Staff*.
One might assume they'd be the most docile:
as their leader, I controlled their fate.
But many a revered leader has faced a bloody coup,
exiled to some second-rate city,
never to return.

The third lion — *Community*, wildly unpredictable,
one day accepting food gently from my fingers,
the next day, leaving me with only single digits.

Caretakers are wise to not divide their time in thirds —
each beast requires absolute attention,
or they'll darken with indignation.
Better to leap back and forth, attending to their needs,
making each feel you are theirs alone.

It's a mistake to see oneself as a lion tamer.
That's the beginning of the end;
one may not tame the untamable.
This is more Serengeti than Siegfried and Roy.
We are merely stewards, providing aid
for a few years of their immortal lives.

We dote on the lions.
We are thrilled when they are thriving.
We stand ready to dispense all they desire,
even if it's ourselves.

Swearing In

The firefighter recruits
beam in new dress blues
that will shrink through the decades.
Parents, girlfriends, boyfriends,
cherishing from folding chairs.

It's swearing-in day. I'm glowing
as if the Buddha brushed by.
My sole role: introduce the Fire Chief
to orchestrate the badge pinning.
My soul full.

Called to serve, to help,
they fear fiery enclosed spaces,
few paths of retreat.
Unaware of the real dangers:
the unending hours
in dorms away from loved ones,
away from their progeny
with plastic red helmets.

Decades before, it was horse, buggy, hose.
Now their steeds are rolling hospitals.
They dismount to hook up the EKG
or deliver the Narcan dose.

You may not like Dalmatians,
red diesel engines,
or even mustaches,
but let me tell you, you will like them
when your mother is lifted from her fall,
your father hauled to the hospital just in time.
Another few minutes, I was told,
and he wouldn't have made it.

Ribbon Cutting

All you need is a pack of photographers
and scissors
the size of a Volkswagen.

Forgotten are the unforeseen delays,
the last-minute influx of cash
filched from a future project.

The groundbreaking, so long ago —
the choreographed scoop of dirt,
shovels spray-painted gold.

A distant memory — the general contractor
who was hell to work with,
the architect who wouldn't stop meddling.

Long gone — the hazardous waste,
trucked away by the hooded safety suits
to who-remembers-where.

Lost to time — the now-retired staff
who had the original dream,
who planted and watered the seed.

The 14 public meetings, now dimming.
The quarreling agencies. The endless
testimony for and against.

Cameras flashing,
we crowd around the red ribbon,
beaming with amnesia.

Grandmayor

for Albert J. Boro

The mayor at my office door —
Churchillian, minus the scowl —
gently eases into the chair opposite me.
There goes 45 minutes of my life.

He has served the city for 36 years.
I'm the new assistant city manager,
still asking for directions downtown.

Soon, I cherish his drop-bys
to share a chapter or two of local lore
as if I were touring Lincoln's home
and the gangly one himself strolls in,
chats for a spell, hands me smoky coffee
from old man Folgers' shoppe up the street.

My parents had parents,
but I never had a grandfather.
The mayor teaches me: slow down, listen.
Even on my manic days.
He spins Tolkien epics
from downtown's battles,
after the big department stores fled,
tails tucked,
to the safety of the suburbs.

This week, he brought the train to the North Bay.
He's built temples for immigrants, not kings.
Maybe the Golden Gate Bridge too,
but that was before my time.

Sure, he had real children, real grandchildren,
but still took in this newbie,
looking for a landing spot,
a temporary refuge,
plotting my next career conquest.

At times, he likens our city to Camelot,
a golden age, full of promise,
which made me the fuzzy-cheeked Arthur
looking for a sword to pull.

A couple decades on — this city my home,
my children's home —
time falling
like a rose petal to soil.
Eight of us in thin white gloves,
straining to hoist his forever bed
up and down the steep church steps.

Eight men sweating through wool suits,
carrying a heavy weight.
Me — lifting him, for a change.

Pronouns

Something's afoot in the footer.
The signature block — a tiny thumbprint of letters,
world's shortest autobiography,
above the inspirational quote,
above the bureaucratic-sounding title,
staking its claim rooted to your name.

Proud of the *he theys* and *they shes* and *they thems*.
Planting your footer flag.
A tiny amenity proclaiming identity.

My Favorite Resident

You startled the retail cashier
with your cheer for the sales tax.
No one had ever done that before.

You knew that it meant a paramedic when you call,
the librarian always ready to help,
the lifeguard giving swim lessons.

It was your arm that shot up
when the city sought neighborhood volunteers
for the green committee.
You made t-shirts that said "Carbon Crushers,"
lightened your city's touch on the Earth.

My first day as city manager, you popped into my office,
not to complain, but to ask how you can help.
You never dug into a position
without planting seeds of other possibilities.

Your species is going extinct,
replaced by the us versus them'ers,
hoisting their banner of "I win if you lose."

I dreamt last night that you came to me
as the Greek Goddess of Municipal Civility.
You granted me three wishes
before fading back into the stars.
Then, everyone truly valued others' opinions.
The only marginalized community was hate,
and all the potholes had been filled.

Waking up, I mused you would've urged me,
on that last wish, to stretch a little harder.

Song to My Local Government People

You are my people:
local government toilers,
wicked problem foilers.

I'll take ten of you randomly
and we can crack any crisis,
slash the tangled forest of discord.
Instead of machetes, we'll use a whiteboard.

We the unsung
but never unstung,
persisting and forging forward
to help, to solve, to innovate.
Together we will celebrate.

We are seldom seen but always see —
what does the community want to be?

We are not expectant spectators.
We are in the arena,
sometimes warrior,
sometimes ballerina.

My people — sister, brother,
truly known,
only to each other.

Part 2

Colleagues: Can't Work With 'Em, Can't Work Without 'Em

A Conversation Between the Library and Recreation Departments on the Eve of Their Merger

We are the library, the keepers of knowledge,
the kerosene lamp illuminating
yellowing pages of wisdom and wonder.

And we are recreation, they retorted,
the health of the spirit, the thrill of competition,
we are fun itself.

Fun? the library snorts.
You sit in the back of the class, the dumb jock
making fart sounds for laughs.

And you, library, you're the acne-addled bookworm,
wearing a t-shirt with the periodic table,
wondering why you're dateless for the prom.

Well, at least we don't charge for our services,
like a common prostitute, sneers the library.
Here, knowledge is free to enlighten all.

Our services are so beloved, gushes recreation,
people are happy to pay.
And we don't bankrupt the city.

The library shrugs and sighs: Can we at least agree
on the city manager's foolishness
in forcing this union?

Yes, replies recreation, but let's delay this debate.
I'm off to teach the beginners French
class at the rec center.

Definitely, says the library,
I have to dash
to lead our weekly Spanish immersion hike.

Perhaps we should grab a drink later.

The Government Zoo

The Millennial and Gen Z speakers' panel,
on how to make City Hall fun,
urges "Take Your Interns to the Zoo Day."

My earliest career mentors, way back in the 1980s,
hijack my mind, their voices shaking me
with their fervor to find fault.

> Ha! the voices scoff, a chorus of scorn.
> Imagine reading that headline:
> *Taxpayer Money Spent on Playdate at Zoo!*
>
> And this "work to live, not live to work" nonsense —
> this is serious work,
> endless responsibilities.

I strain to hear the panelists, something
about a new world order of disorder,
an era that feels low trust and unjust,
City Hall staff stressing empathy and joy.

> Joy? the inner voices snort in retort.
> Isn't that what a paycheck is for?
>
> Better to slog out your years until retirement.
> Issues growing more complicated?
> Just put in more hours. Sacrifice.

I implore the voices to grab their briefcases and scram.
Good riddance!

Work with joy? Handling problems
but not hanging them around your neck
until you droop like a shepherd's staff?
I hear zoo tickets are two for one on Tuesdays.

Intern Wanted

You showed up at City Hall
as if in a basket left on the steps,
just over 20 years old,
but still a newborn to us.

We asked you to propel us into the 21st century,
paying you like it was the 20th.
Your title: "Intern,"
French for "stay quiet and get coffee."

But you were the intern who could turn minds
and in turn, hearts,
in your jet-black Warby Parker glasses,
a pile of pumps stashed under your desk,
your energy — endless.

We drowned you in paper,
but you made origami and moved everything online.
We gave you crises after crises —
you fashioned sublime policies.

You grew to Analyst I, Analyst II, and then
a title not even a mother could love:
Senior Management Analyst.

You and your merry band of Millennials,
winning over the most jaded
with your viral enthusiasm.
We would redesign all our services
with your plethora of Post-it notes.

Next, you were called
Director of Digital Service and Open Government,
a mouthful that meant Chief Reimaginer of Everything.
We had the country talking, marveling
at our triumphs.

Then, the invisible hand of the Big Virus
picked you up and set you down someplace else,
as it did for so many.

It was you who birthed us.
Now we long for that cord that bound us,
that allowed us to breathe.

The Great Professor

Most men of his generation would have ignored
or undermined their new, young pup boss,
but this venerable finance director took pity on me.

You know what UAAL is, kid? he inquired.
No, something about United Airlines, I guessed.
He winked, OK, we've got some work to do.

How about GASB? he asked. Do you know GASB 34 or 45?
Oh, yeah, Gatsby I read in high school, I replied,
although I think it took place in the '20s
because they had all those flapper dresses.
He winced, I'm talking about unfunded liability.

I'd never taken accounting,
but I lapped up each financial dish he served.

The oldest staffer at City Hall, he came from another era.
He was childhood friends with the Beach Boys,
when they were actually boys.
I could picture him surfing with the Wilsons,
talking about girls, or more likely,
how much of an ass their dads were.

But now, many decades later,
he didn't quite fit in a modern office,
his run-ins with HR becoming more common.
But to me he was Socrates,
the professor from Dead Poet's Society,
Mr. Holland and his Opus all rolled into one,
like a glorious angel sent from heaven
to teach me tax increment financing,
and how to review bond indenture documents.

I had nothing to offer in return.
I took, as a child, without any reciprocity.
Oh, yes, "reciprocity," the act of linking together
multiple defined benefit pension systems —
he taught me that too.

If only we could repay the gentle guidance we receive.
Is it something, at least, that I think of him often,
barreling down the road in some 1950s heaven?
Him at the wheel, Brian Wilson riding shotgun,
belting songs at the top of their lungs,
teenage Rhonda and her cousin Barbara Ann in the back seat,
the Pacific appearing in the distance,
in their four-speed, dual-quad, Positraction 409.

Labor of Love

It's all about preparation and strategy,
as if you're going into battle, the firefighter explains,
on that suffocating summer day in 1999,
smoke flattening the air.

When the alarm goes off,
you respond —
veins bursting with effort,
sweat like water gushing from a hose.

It's all about people's lives and livelihood.
You attack from every angle,
hoping to carry the victory flag
at the end of the day.

Yes, today is the day —
the alarm has gone off:
the retirement plan is *overfunded*,
and public safety pensions are on the agenda.

The Mountain

He's a numbers guy,
king of the city's finances,
sees the world in binary — correct or incorrect,
the ledger neatly tallied.
A bit of a loner, preferring older friends
such as Euclid or Archimedes.
Not loved by his peers,
who want him to open up
and shake the city's wallet a bit harder.

You float in, shattering that stereotype:
Venus with a spreadsheet,
a woman finance director composing
at a whiteboard on a Friday afternoon,
rocking a vintage AC/DC t-shirt,
dreaming up the city of the future,
taking us there with you.

You, nicknamed Mountain,
for your enduring spirit and might.
Our laughter echoes off your hillsides,
sprouting wildflowers of affection.
Rivers of strife may carve your resolve,
but it would take centuries.

Your spirit outshines all you've been:
a little girl fleeing a war,
a wife suddenly a widow,
a mother losing a child.
You've looked Death in the eye,
your eyes aglow with goodness
as Death skulks off ashamed.

You find ways to heal,
yet beyond that, to heal others,
to sit with their pain — be their mountain.
You continue to love, be loved,
learning you can carry many friends,
even an entire city.

And with all that,
as we amble through the woods,
you ask *me* for logic
to restore your faith in humanity.

I ramble — "the youth is our future"
or some such platitude —
as all the evidence in the world
walks alongside me.

Haiku for Retiring City Planner Bob Brown

Long from now goes Brown,
and St. Peter says to him,
You got a permit?

Department Director Annual Retreat

for my beloved Department Directors

I drive to the coast to my staff retreat,
morning sun outshined by fog.
Each mile, I shed the mundane, the temporal.
First, my briefcase sails out the window, then my tie.
Next, my woolen suit of armor — won't be needing that.

The remote inn appears through the mist.
I enter the meeting room — simply myself.
Here we will spend the next day and a half,
reimagining what it means to be city staff,
reimagining ourselves.

The stirring magic starts to swirl,
first slowly seeping in as if through the vents,
and then spiraling through each of us
as we tell our stories, listen to each other, dream.

Who are we, who do we want to be,
what does this moment in time demand,
how will we greet it with grace,
always leading with love?

By afternoon's end,
everyone has shed their needless layers.
We sit in a circle — skeletons with a brain and heart.
The challenges back in the office abound,
but we now face them as one.

At dinner, some children point and laugh
at the table of a dozen rowdy skeletons,
but their parents hush them, tell them to look away.

We don't begrudge them —
who could understand our fierce bond?
As the wine warmly flows, some settles in our brain,
but most pools in our hearts.

We retire to the inn's dimly lit lounge,
talking for hours, music blaring
from a plastic Hello Kitty speaker,
as if it were the sound system at the Hollywood Bowl.

Some of the skeletons chat, others play games,
and I have found the pool table.
How much easier it is to shoot pool,
when you rely simply on bone and wooden cue.

Around this time, our brains have put on their pajamas
and blown out the candle, so we are merely hearts
held snug in our skeleton frames.

Finally, we release even our skeletons.
Now it is just our hearts talking to each other,
speaking a tender language
understood only by linked hearts.

The next morning for breakfast,
most of us have slipped back into our skin suits.
What would the inn's other guests think
if they came across a room full of hearts,
eating chocolate croissants, sliced fruit?

In a few hours, we finish the work of the retreat,
embrace, take a photo. We'll do this again next year.
To hold us till then, we stuff our pockets, purses,
and the inn's complimentary tote bag
with all the retreat magic we can carry.

As my car floats back home, the ocean behind it,
I feel renewed, alive, in a hurry to get back to City Hall.
I stop only once, to search in the tall grasses
for my briefcase and tie.

Partners

for Cristine, my Assistant City Manager

Batman and Robin — the obvious reply
when asked for the typical relationship
between city manager and assistant city manager.
There is the caped crusader with a shadowy past,
and the loyal and skillful sidekick,
happy to call shotgun every time Batman
slides in behind the steering wheel of the Batmobile.

But that's not us, we've been told.
Our staff calls us Spock and Kirk.
But wait, why am I Spock? I bristle.
As the city manager, shouldn't I be Kirk?
But staff just rolls their eyes —
my Spock-ness is undeniable.

Everything I do — based on logic and planning,
calculating moves, countermoves,
designing a reasoned plan for every response.

And you, the strong, take-no-prisoners, charismatic leader
always jumping into the fray,
happy to boldly go where few women have gone before.

The bridge needed both of us
to get through these many years,
one national or global crisis after the other.
You and I, the perfect recipe of creativity and resilience.
Just make it two Kirks or two Spocks at the helm,
and watch the dysfunction ensue.

Soon you will have your turn as captain,
Kirk resuming the role's proper position,
and I will tend my garden on Vulcan,
gladly calculating the exact percentage likelihood
that my tulips will bloom this year.

Part 3

Getting Through the Day

Putting on My Thick Skin

Crowd gathering in the city council chambers,
waiting in the worn movie theater style seats,
clutching their garbage bills,
rehearsing their upcoming rants.

They see me enter in my off-the-rack gray suit,
tie garroting my neck,
as I greet one or two of my staff,
approach my seat at the dais
beside the city council, my bosses.
A typical scene played out
in every city in America.

Inside my head: a different movie,
a montage of images through space and time.
My entrance — majestic and jubilant.
I arrive at City Hall in a gilded Roman chariot,
white horses barely restrained, nostrils flaring.
A mighty leap and I land
at the base of the monumental steps.

Now I am Rocky. I bound up the stairs,
the great hope of the working class,
triumphant trumpet blasting *Gonna Fly Now*.
I vault the final three steps,
fists pumped to the heavens.

The lobby becomes my on-deck circle,
bases loaded in the bottom of the ninth.
I approach the plate, my walk-up music blaring,
Freddie Mercury belts *We Will Rock You*
through the shrill lobby speakers
now transformed into a Marshall stack.

My jersey recast as a suit as I enter the chambers.
Taking my seat, I'm transported
behind the desk in the Oval Office.
I'm about to address the American people,
the fate of democracy hanging in the balance.
The cameras switch on, three…two…one…

Pressing my microphone button jars me
back to the present.
Finally, I speak: Thank you, Madame Mayor,
I'd like to introduce staff to present
our report on the annual garbage rate study.

City Manager Gulliver

The puny archers fire arrow after arrow
but they are no match for me.
They bounce off my leathery skin,
a mere annoyance.

Though I'm giant to them, they attack.
One archer launches homelessness, then mental illness.
Another lets fly injustice and racial inequity,
but they glance off me as easily as the others.
Here comes political extremism, and now, violent protests.
Their ropes of pollution and poverty,
mere spiderwebs that I brush off.

But I am not Gulliver; I'm the bull in the ring,
charging the matador's red tasseled cape.
The pikes and banderillas of the crises
stain my hide, red streaked and wet.

First enraging me, but slowly, with each one,
weakening, weakening.
A dull sound in my ears, getting louder.
The roar of the crowd now deafening.

Version Control

So timely to meet my future wife at age 26.
You wouldn't want to make a life
with versions 1 through 25.

It got particularly glitchy around version 16,
I'll blame the hormones,
but you'd also cast your eyes downward
to your phone if you walked past
versions 18 through 22 at an airport.

Similarly, I'm glad I waited until I was 47
to take on the demanding duty
of city manager,
rewiring the circuits of government.

If I had started in my 20s,
I would have been quoting hair metal bands
in my staff reports.
If I had started in my 30s,
I would have been mostly asleep in my chair,
because that's when the twins were young.

Version 47 was expensive
and didn't come with much of a warranty,
but at least most of the bugs were fixed.

Informal Authority

In my dream I fidget in the tiny office chair,
the city attorney lecturing me, the city manager,
as if from Lincoln's marble throne.

Scolding arguments, one after another,
twisting through decades of case law.
The advice: no, no, and hell no.

If I want to fly the pride month flag at City Hall
I'd have to also allow the Nazi flag
or Beelzebub's flaming flag from the gates of hell.

I hoist the pride flag personally,
for each of the thirty days of June.

Then, I obliterate the ceremonial flagpole
with the cold rolled steel of a Ford F350 bumper.

I'm guessing it will take us
exactly 11 months to repair.

Like Talking to a Tree

I walk wounded into the redwoods,
straining to carry all I must show them:
when I was wronged, my weakening resolve,
the challenging chores of running a city.

I lay my pile of angst against their shaggy trunks —
maybe this time they will listen, share their wisdom.
"I am so miserable," I yell upwards, arms outstretched.
"Show me the way, O Wise Ones!"

Silence, as always.
Just gently swaying in the wind.
Sedate, unconcerned,
not to be bothered.

They are so useless,
merely turning sun into energy,
storing the earth's carbon,
modeling resilience,
and refusing to answer my questions.

I sulk off, deaf to their divine chorus.

Run the City Like a Business

Run the city like a business,
the new councilmember orders me,
the city manager.
You mean like Blockbuster?
Enron?
Lehman Brothers?

Shall we pluck "quality of life" from the mission statement
and plug in "maximize profit"?

Who'll pay the true cost to replace streets,
the miles of rusted metal pipes?
Only top donors allowed in the city pool?
Will the rescued family pay
for the firefighter's back surgery?
Will criminals pay for their arrest?

Or, maybe you mean the solar company
living off government grants.
The housing developer
feeding on tax credits.

The librarian's not profitable,
so no need for lifelong learning.
The crossing guard's not profitable,
so to hell with child safety.
Or better yet, let's treat the crosswalk like a bridge —
collect their lunch money for the toll.

You've convinced me.
Let's talk CEO salary and stock options.

Little Free Library

The little free library
with the blue frame and orange door,
your gift to the world
in front of your comely cottage.
O patron of the arts.
O dispenser of charity.

A 20-inch by 24-inch shrine
in the city's right-of-way.
You care nothing for utility access,
permits of encroachment.
Did Andrew Carnegie always get permission?
Does the Library of Congress consider easements?

It may be free, but decidedly not a free-for-all,
your taped, handwritten note
proudly stating your rules:
"Please — No self-published books
and no political propaganda.
Thank You."

Truth or Dare, Frigidaire?

I always put my lunch on the right side
of the office mini-fridge's lowest shelf;
my daily protein drink in the door pocket.

And yet, you violate my sovereign territory,
time and time again,
as if there were no refrigerator rules.

It started innocently enough, with your baby carrots
perched up against my salad,
but when your celery stalks invaded,
wilting for over a week,
I was at wit's end.

Yes, the geopolitical dynamics of refrigerator control
are complex, vacillating.
Your UFOs (Unidentified Food-like Objects)
smell of corpse flower.
Your hand-scrawled notes
remind people that their mother does not work here,
but for heaven's sake,
why is your Reddi-wip in my door pocket again?

And, what the hell, do you use Reddi-wip every day?
Who uses Reddi-wip every day?
Go ahead, move my protein drink again,
just one more time — go ahead, I dare you.

Covert Maneuvers at Safeway

I strike in the cover of darkness,
slipping into the grocery store camouflaged,
not a city manager but a commando behind enemy lines.
My mission: get in, get out undetected,
safely securing my groceries.

Inside, fluorescent lights blasting,
meddling with my subterfuge.
I shrink further into my jacket,
eyes darting for known threats.
I am a raid specialist, master of stealth.

Aisle three looks clear — I make a beeline,
dodging behind a greeting card rack
to maintain my invisibility.
Where he came from, I cannot say,
but he is already talking to me.
Aren't you the city manager? I saw you on TV.
I brace myself — will it be barking dogs, potholes, graffiti,
the need for more stop signs, fewer stop signs,
the recent rash of stolen catalytic converters?

After fifteen minutes vowing repeatedly
to follow up, I am freed.
I focus, take some deep breaths, start reconnaissance.
School board member on aisle five,
Rotary president near the meat counter,
local realtor in frozen foods.
Zigzagging, I evade them all and fill my cart.
I am an elite trooper once again.
I can do this.

And then:
I think she's that super-user on Nextdoor.
Maybe she won't know me.
Oh, I know you, she exclaims.
Cover blown.

She looks down at my cart,
judging my Cool Ranch Doritos and Miller Lite,
tsk-tsk expression forming on her face.
She assaults me about the lack of crossing guards,
teenagers speeding down her street,
her neighbor's unnecessary addition
blocking her view of the hills.

You'd think strangers would be the worst,
but it's actually friends — they feel entitled,
having the inside track, confident
their complaints are no imposition
at 9 p.m. on a Sunday night.
Hey! Good to see you buddy.
What's the city doing about homelessness?
Aren't those new apartments going to cause gridlock?
Didn't you see the couch dumped at the park?

I'm on the move again. Slinking around,
loitering behind a pyramid of cantaloupes
until the checkout line is clear.
At last, I slip back into the comforting shadows
of the parking lot. A guy from the Elks Club
is looking at his phone near the cart return.
My cart will not be returned today.

At last, arriving back at home,
my heart drops to the floor mats,
to the oil stains on the driveway.
Had I forgotten something?

White Vests

I slip into the white vest,
in the third month of 2020,
city manager morphing into emergency director.
In the vest, I buy masks by the truckload,
turn streets into restaurants,
ban rent hikes and evictions.
My city staff now disaster workers.

If you wore your city's white vest,
you know it wasn't all triumph.
It wasn't just pride in leading your team
through a herculean task.
It wasn't always knowing what's right
and guiding staff there.

Yes, you kept order, kept people pointed
in the right direction, kept trying,
but it was like holding a single playing card
and trying to guess the other 51.

Future city managers won't know,
can't know what it felt like.
The unknown time horizon, suffocating
like being below the surface of the water,
kicking upwards, the light getting no brighter,
seeing you are not surfacing —
in fact, may drown.
Thinking it would be days, then weeks, months,
but it was years.

Early on, when there is no information,
we flock together
managing the crisis side by side.
A week or two later, we try to manage
a global catastrophe sitting alone
in front of a computer screen,
medical advice changing daily.

We set up drive-through testing,
dole out grants to businesses and renters,
care for the children of the caregivers,
feed the homebound
and those without homes,
move City Hall online.
911 calls being answered, as always,
in person and hands-on.

Who will believe we closed parks and playgrounds?
Who will believe we removed the rims at basketball courts,
like a dystopian world that'd outlawed play?

We pray for a vaccine,
pray for no outbreaks at nursing homes,
publish weekly messages of resiliency and hope
as if our city were under heavy bombing.

The future will judge the white vests
for not doing enough, or in the right places,
or for the right people.
They'll look at cold metrics and pass judgment.

The white vests will know
we did everything we could,
that it was like trying to orderly manage
the slow-motion explosion of the world.

Punch Drunk

The first time I was sucker punched,
I totally deserved it.
I shouldn't have brought nunchucks to a fistfight.
I know that now.

The second time I was sucker punched,
I was kissing my then-girlfriend on the subway.
Was that one racially motivated?
I'll never know.

The third time I was sucker punched,
I thought I could break through severe mental illness
with my sincere compassion and smile.
That was naive of me.

All the other times I have been sucker punched,
it was as city manager and by events like the pandemic,
recessions, an employee dying on the job,
beloved staff leaving,
a spike in 9-1-1 calls, lawsuits,
pedestrians killed in intersections,
staff behaving badly, wildfires, floods.

Better to get hit in the face.

Part 4

Dreaming On

The Mayor Has a Hammer

No doubt you can picture the mayor,
country club insignia on his sweater vest,
every hair gelled into place.
But you may overlook his leather tool belt,
full of empty holsters, pockets, snaps of every kind,
utterly purposeless, as it simply holds
a hammer.

The hammer dangles in a place of pride,
an only child, basking in importance.
The hammerhead reverently polished
by the mayor who loves this tool so much
there is no room for any other on his belt,
or in his heart.

The mayor will charm you to get what he desires,
whatever the crucial civic goal of the day.
And you may fall under his spell
should you find yourself enraptured
by tales of his tennis triumphs,
that weekend's exploits at the club.
If the incantation fails, out comes the hammer.

Look closely to see faint stains of blood
of those cast aside by the hammer's rage.
Though the redness has mainly been polished away,
its shadow darkly whispers dreadful deeds.

Crafting the best civic policy, though, is complex,
requiring an array of precision tools
that would make a modern dental tray blush in its crudeness.

Sometimes solving a societal ill
merely requires needle-nose pliers or a metric wrench.
Others demand the tiniest pentalobe screwdriver
or high torque spline socket.

But the mayor has a hammer,
his arms spread triumphantly at the bow of the yacht
as the sun dances off his silver hair.

Open Time for Public Comment

Though my title is city manager,
I'm more of a community helper —
just like Hamburger Helper
but with more education and less gluten.

Harmonizing opposing goals,
untwisting conflict, untangling knots,
walking hand in hand with the community,
conjuring the future together,
making the city's loftiest dreams
dance into reality.

Me — wrapped in the city flag,
gently weeping tears of pride.
Why then, at the council meeting,
must you use your two minutes
calling for my head?

Quietly Listening to Public Comment at the City Council Meeting

As you boil over,
steaming your accusations and demands,
growling opposition
to the outdoor music series at the local bar,
I feel genuine curiosity why is it you chose to live
in the largest city in the county,
and then chose the downtown
of the largest city in the county,
and then chose the main street of the downtown
of the largest city in the county,
and then decided to complain
about noise levels and decibel readings.

Perhaps the suburbs would be a better place for you —
but no, the neighbor will have a barking dog,
or children squealing on a backyard swing set.
Perhaps a remote farm is the best place for you —
but no, crows can be pretty loud in the morning,
and the midnight coyotes with their 12-part harmonies.

The Municipal Performance Evaluation as a Love Sonnet

How do I rate thee? Let me count the ways.
You're the highest performer on my team,
well-liked by all staff, it really does seem.
My hearty love for you goes on for days.

Sure, you've stolen office supplies, my beau.
Some steal paper clips, but you — the pool car.
I agree driving to Vegas was "not very far."
With my loving care, you will learn and grow.

Your Super Bowl party was a real rager.
Not authorized, but the most people we had
in the council chambers this year, I'd wager.

I can overlook all of this, my friend,
but you ate my beloved pastry from the fridge.
Your keys, please, by 5 p.m. For you — the end.

Tilting at Windmills

Once I cite the inarguable wisdom,
he says, of shrinking their planned pension
in trade for a raise today,
they will embrace my genius.

I highly doubt that, Mayor Quixote,
but you go right ahead.

Let us forge forward, young Sancho Panza,
he declares. I will show you the way!

Of course, sir, I say, eyes cast downward,
but give me a moment to gather my basket
to pick up your head
when it rolls past me.

Later, the head looks up at me from the basket —
still that serene pool
of confidence and aplomb.

Or was there one small wrinkle,
above the left eye,
that revealed a sudden moment
of recognition and surprise.

Municipal Drinking Games

Everyone takes a shot, each time:

Someone at the city council meeting
uses an acronym.

A resident says — "I'm not against development,
just this project."

The local gadfly exceeds the allowed time
to speak at the podium.

The person with the parking ticket
says they were only there for a few minutes.

Someone says they are stepping down
to spend more time with family.

The newspaper's headline
is unnecessarily incendiary.

You get a complaint about the library's
drag queen story time.

The Municipal Code refers to the city manager as
he.

A.H. (After Humans)

I wonder what cockroaches will call the era after humans.
Will they simply use A.H.
or something more mocking and derisive?
Of course, we'll never know, and it won't be in English anyway,
but rather cockroach dialect, just as complex
with all its hisses, whistles, buzzing, and chirping.

On Earth for some 320 million years,
they're exquisitely designed
to thrive on a burning planet.

Will their history teachers bother reciting lessons
of climate change, wildfires and hurricanes, oil wars?
Will they add that local governments did every possible
tiny thing within their finite power
as national governments fiddled,
took turns impeaching each other, and worse?

Will their philosophers and poets decry, or just forget,
about the era when they were forced
to live below ground, and in drains —
before their benevolent rule from cockroach castles,
the pyramids replaced with colossal perfect spheres
rolled into place by their ancient friends, the dung beetles.

The beetles and other A.H. species will have
deep admiration for the cockroaches,
builders of great societies,
of cities steered by their blueprints for the future,
rather than countries with immutable constitutions.

If we knew the glory of their upcoming rule,
would we have still treated them with disdain,
squishing with impunity?

Humans have a long history of switching allegiances
to the conqueror nearing victory.
Maybe now is the time to endear yourself
to the future glitterati.

Hollow Man

> *after T.S. Eliot's "The Hollow Men"*

Wayne schemes safely on the city's sidelines,
launching blistering attack ads,
rumor mills, smear campaigns.
His political action committee
unleashing last-minute hit pieces,
aiming at whoever displeases him,
smacking his lips with delicious destruction.

What now — he's entering the arena?
Wayne himself running for city council?
How utterly delightful!

This is the way Wayne ends,
this is the way Wayne ends,
this is the way Wayne ends,
not with a bang but a whimper.

Not Your Turn to Speak

As the massive horde of protesters amassed
that hot, late spring day,
the leaders wanted nothing to do with us,
didn't need us, didn't want us,
even told the police chief that he,
and the rest of us *government types*,
could march from the rear,
if we had to be there at all.

We had expected a few grannies,
maybe some college kids,
but it filled city blocks.
Many hundreds of bodies
full of purpose, like a tidal wave,
surging from street to street,
roaring messages on oversized signs:
Black Lives Matter,
Remember George Floyd,
I Can't Breathe,
No Justice, No Peace.

There is a time for discourse,
a time for reconciliation.
This was not that time.
This was a time for marching, chanting,
kneeling, saying the names,
demanding justice, accountability,
showing solidarity,
fighting back.

And yet, you, the white 70-year-old Councilman,
clad in your silk lined suit,
convertible Mercedes parked nearby,
demand the microphone
on the brick steps of City Hall,
to tell people how it is.

And you speak,
and speak, and speak.
What valor, what restraint
it must have taken to allow you to do so.
Such that has been relied on
for hundreds of years.

Don't Run for City Council

Don't run for city council
if you only aspire to higher office,
or to kill the latest development plan,
or to ensure no change at all,
preferring that time stops
with your historic arrival.

Don't run if you're anti-tax but gripe
about shabby streets and parks,
or those who want to slash the budget,
despite never having scanned it.
Don't run, please, because you were flattered
by the encouragement of your fellow Rotarians.

Don't run if you're intoxicated by your own voice,
or to finally have a venue
where people have to listen to you.
Don't run if everyone else on the city council
already looks just like you.

Make way instead for the innovators,
the dreamers, the romantics
who will the city into the future,
who prefer the virtuous path
over what's politically painless.
Those optimists who inhale conflict
and exhale unity,
partnering with city staff,
always breathing as one.

Run for office if you've studied the city,
care deeply for it and all its people —
if you can't tell the difference
between the crisscrossing roads
and your own veins and arteries.

Candidates

I'm telling you,
that city council candidate:
so much smarter than her opponent.

It's like Athena, Goddess of Wisdom, against
Jennifer, Goddess of Conventional Wisdom.

Help Wanted: City Manager (Applicants Apply Within)

But first, look within. Want five or more elected bosses doling out conflicting direction? Relish whiplashing from team building into hostile union negotiations, or pinballing from emergency response to housing crisis to failing infrastructure to social services?

Can you decisively lead the troops during a disaster? Get a kick out of the media tracking your worst moments? Can you look deadpan into a camera and tackle the most outlandish questions?

Want to be on the clock 24/7 and lose sleep over that day's dilemma? Will you carry your city's population on your shoulders? Can you shrug off that everyone thinks the mayor runs the city?

Benefits: You get to make people's lives better every day, build a team as tight as a military unit under fire, feel the honor of leading those saving lives and sailing into the seas of noble challenges. You will have a life worth living.

Compensation: You'll be paid well, but no matter the amount, the community will say you're a lazy bureaucrat and don't deserve it.

Notes

Part 1: For the Love of Public Service

Confessions of an Accomplishoholic
As local government staff, we are always setting goals and objectives and implementing plans and strategies of every kind. The pursuit of results can be exhilarating and addictive. At times, it is important to remember to slow down and reflect and enjoy the work rather than just bouncing to the next task.

The Giver
We change the course of people's lives when we offer them a new job. It sometimes feels a massive responsibility. And it can affect not just the new hire but their entire family. There is always risk involved as to whether it will be right for them and for the local government. Are we responsible for whom we hire and what happens to them afterward professionally? Personally?

Tragedy of the Commoners
The tragedy of the commons theory explains that individuals with access to a public resource (the commons) make self-interested decisions despite the negative impacts for others. Local governments are the curators of the commons, working for the overall good.

City Hall
When traveling anywhere in the country and passing a City Hall, I would say to my kids, "That's where Daddy works." I am equally proud of every City Hall. I can enter any one of them and find like-minded people who care deeply about their communities. When I walk through the doors of any City Hall today, I feel I am home.

City Council Chambers
The City Council Chambers is the living room of democracy. All are welcome to provide their input as vociferously as they like. It is a place that can feel orchestrated but where anything can happen. The history of the city was made there and its future will be birthed from there as well.

Pride of Lions
The three-legged stool of city management is the city council, city staff, and the community. They each could easily consume all of one's time. The city manager must meet the needs of each or be eaten.

Swearing In
There are moments of rejuvenation for city managers — being at swearing-in ceremonies, ribbon cuttings, meritorious conduct awards — that seep in and remind you why you do this work. It's important to cherish those moments.

Ribbon Cutting
A ribbon cutting for a new city facility or infrastructure always makes for a happy day. It is a good time to set aside all the challenges that preceded the celebration and just focus on the shining new project and its value in the community.

Grandmayor
Mayor Boro was one of many elected officials who taught me that mayors and council members are just regular people. They may wield great power in a very formal setting but may also be a dad, mom, or even a grandfather. I miss him coming into my office, saying "Hey, kid!" and sitting down for a long chat.

Pronouns
This poem notices that it is becoming increasingly common

for individuals to let others know which pronouns they prefer to have used when referencing the individual. This can be a controversial topic that can bring up passionate generational or political differences — or it can just be a simple sign of respect.

My Favorite Resident
I can't overstate how heartwarming it is to work with this kind of resident. I wish for your city to be entirely made up of favorite residents.

Song to My Local Government People
This love poem is inspired by Theodore Roosevelt's 1910 speech popularly known as *The Man in the Arena*, which reads in part: "It is not the critic who counts; not the man who points out how the strong man stumbles, or where the doer of deeds could have done them better. The credit belongs to the man who is actually in the arena..." Gendered language aside, all local government professionals are in the arena and we must be adaptable to every situation — sometimes we must fight, sometimes dance, but we always do it together.

Part 2: Colleagues: Can't Work With 'Em, Can't Work Without 'Em

A Conversation Between the Library and Recreation Departments on the Eve of Their Merger
Departments evolve over time and mergers can be controversial with passionate voices in support or opposition. This poem plays with the idea that departments may have more in common than the overused stereotypes at the surface. Groups that feel in opposition to each other are better off looking for commonalities.

The Government Zoo
With the pandemic, Great Resignation, and demographic changes, so many of the old rules of local government are now obsolete. While that might be scary for some, it has been long overdue for others. Today, we need to create environments of strong mental health and self-care to foster engaged and resilient employees who love their careers doing meaningful work.

Intern Wanted
A child who grows up and leaves home can be a triumph but also can be a brutal loss for the parent. This also happens in the workplace, when staff you've nurtured and promoted over time wind up taking a job elsewhere. You still may be able to visit them, but it is never the same as when they lived under your roof.

The Great Professor
I've found local government employees to be fantastically giving of their knowledge and expertise to newcomers, when approached with respect and appreciation. You learn so much more on the job than can be taught in four years of college. Our colleagues become our teachers.

Labor of Love
I have a deep admiration and affection for firefighters. These are the people who on perhaps the worst day of your life are the ones rushing to you or your family as quickly as possible to help. Also, they have a reputation of being relentless labor negotiators. In this poem, I poke fun at that relentlessness in 1999 when CalPERS — the nation's largest public pension fund, managing retirement benefits for California's public employees — was deemed super-funded, setting the stage for higher pension benefits.

The Mountain
Though local government employees can get lumped together in less-than-flattering stereotypes, they are fantastically unique and special people who care deeply about the world. If only everyone could see beyond the governmental titles and roles to the genuine humans within — they would be amazed at the brilliance, empathy, resilience, and drive.

Haiku for Retiring City Planner Bob Brown
Unlike the real "Brown" this poem was written for, a small minority of city planners can get drunk with regulatory power and permitting authority. I sometimes wonder how they would feel if the tables were turned.

Department Director Annual Retreat
It is almost always helpful to connect as a team and build culture by having an offsite retreat. For the highest functioning teams, it can be a profound experience. When those high functioning teams are made up of humans who genuinely support and care for each other, the experience can be transcendent.

Partners
The city manager and assistant city manager relationship is a special one. This poem was written about a year before my retirement as city manager as I thought about passing the baton to my assistant. It plays with how two individuals can form a unique bond based on their complementary strengths and personalities.

Part 3: Getting Through the Day

Putting on My Thick Skin
Government executives have always been told they need a thick skin to be a barrier against those that will oppose you, criticize, threaten, etc. Sometimes you have it already; sometimes you need to put it on, like a suit of armor, even for innocuous-sounding topics.

City Manager Gulliver
This poems goes deeper into the notion of thick skin, asking questions like "what is it really" and "is it emotionally healthy?" If you don't feel strong and capable, you can't take on the enormous challenges that come up when running a city. But those same challenges can sometimes make you feel beaten down and questioning your ability to keep doing the work. Maintaining good mental health requires us to regularly check in on ourselves and find ways to recharge and stay passionate about this important work.

Version Control
Sometimes people are in a rush to get to the city manager chair. I often advise people to slow down, learn and grow, and enjoy the various positions and people along the way. The big chair will be there waiting for you when you are ready.

Informal Authority
There are so many rules and constraints for public officials that the subconscious mind is sometimes apt to daydream self-entertaining "what if" scenarios.

Like Talking to a Tree
When things were most stressful in city management, I would go for a long solo hike in the forest, and each time

I would be reminded that the trees persevere and my problems are fleeting. This was quite comforting, because my day-to-day problems shrank in the presence of the great trees that have survived logging, pests, disease, extreme weather, wildfire and so many other hardships. This poem is about someone who hasn't quite learned that lesson yet.

Run the City Like a Business
We've all heard people say that government should run like a business but there are so many services that can't fully recover costs (think homelessness, mental illness, public safety). Also, taxes rarely cover all desired services or the massive costs of infrastructure updates. Funding government is wildly complex, but "running it like a business" makes a great sound bite.

Little Free Library
When I look fondly on these ubiquitous boxes, I am most often thinking about the new sharing economy and neighbors helping neighbors. This poem reveals that, when my better angels are not plucking their harps, I can also get cranky about private structures in the public right-of-way, particularly when they go after authors!

Truth or Dare, Frigidaire?
This poem has a deep hidden meaning. Actually, it doesn't. I think, at one time or another, we all have felt personally violated by the refrigerator antics of our colleagues. It is about time we demand a new constitution to protect our inalienable rights to respectful refrigeration.

Covert Maneuvers at Safeway
I'd like to say this poem comes from a large imagination and I'd never feel this way, but just ask my wife how often I avoided going to the grocery store if you want the truth. City managers are expected to be "on" 24/7, even when

coaching Little League, getting a haircut, or shopping. For those of us more introverted or private, it can sometimes lead to covert maneuvers.

White Vests
When there is a major emergency, local government employees transform into disaster service workers. Those in the Emergency Operations Center (EOC) wear vests showing their roles: white for management, red for operations, blue for planning, yellow for logistics, and green for finance. We practiced and drilled for floods, fires, and earthquakes — but never for a years-long pandemic.

Punch Drunk
If city management is largely an office job, is it odd that managers sometimes use violent language to describe day-to-day feelings? For example: "We took a beating at the council meeting last night," or, "I still have the scars from that neighborhood meeting." This poem is about the stress city managers can feel, particularly from things that go wrong all of the sudden. There are countless joys of city management, but there are also sucker punches.

Part 4: Dreaming On

The Mayor Has a Hammer
I worked under an actual Mayor (Susan) Hammer in my career, but this poem is not about her. It's more of a tongue-in-cheek take on the power of position. When I think about someone's skills in local government, I sometimes picture them with an invisible tool belt — what tools do they bring? City managers work with elected officials of all skill levels. This poem is about the ones with just a hammer. Perhaps there is a certain blissfulness in never having to worry if you selected precisely the right tool.

Open Time for Public Comment
The "open time for public comment" in a city council meeting is when anyone can have a couple minutes or so to say anything they want to. People might be extremely well informed or not informed at all but equally comfortable saying, or sometimes shouting, their opinions. City managers tend to respectfully listen — occasionally longing for the next agenda item.

Quietly Listening to Public Comment at the City Council Meeting
There are three overarching human traits: 1) the capacity for good, 2) the capacity for evil, and 3) the capacity to move next to an existing land use and then emphatically oppose its right to exist. Perhaps the greatest venue for this third human trait is every city council chamber in America.

The Municipal Performance Evaluation as a Love Sonnet
This poem is a variation of an Italian Renaissance Petrarchan sonnet in that it has 14 lines; two subgroups divided into an octave and a sestet; a specific rhyming pattern for the octave (ABBA) and sestet (CDC); about ten syllables per line; and a set-up in the octave that reaches a resolution in the sestet. Performance evaluations can be mundane. You can aid the process with new technology or, perhaps, an 800-year-old form of poetry.

Tilting at Windmills
The relationship between mayor and city manager is complex. You can be partners and simultaneously acknowledge the boss-employee dynamic. There are times to insert yourself, and times to just let things play out on their own. City managers are constantly making this decision.

Municipal Drinking Games
This list could have gone on and on. Even though every jurisdiction is different, there are also shared experiences that create a bond between local government employees. Remember — drink responsibly.

A.H. (After Humans)
No, it's not a poem about cockroaches. This climate change poem encourages one to think about what is within our local government's control when facing a global issue, and what's outside its scope. The bits within our control can feel exhilarating while the sheer magnitude outside of our control can feel demoralizing, frustrating, or even, sometimes, apocalyptic.

Hollow Man
Politics has been called a blood sport, and some people love to sit on the sidelines and throw rocks. It is rare and intriguing when they decide to put themselves out there and run for election. The poem owes its ending to the famous concluding lines of T.S. Eliot's in "The Hollow Men."

Not Your Turn to Speak
This poem explores the role of local government officials in community-initiated actions, such as the protest marches in 2020, and how race can impact what is appropriate. As with most things, it is not just the "what" that is the question, but the "how" and the "why" that can leave more long-lasting impressions.

Don't Run for City Council
There are many motivations to run for office, and so many seem to be tied up in ego rather than a genuine desire to help a community achieve its goals. I'm hoping, if you are an elected official, that you recognize yourself in the second half of the poem rather than the first half.

Candidates
This poem expresses, in the shortest way possible, how we can feel a profound divide between candidates for office and how achingly obvious it sometimes feels in our bones.

Help Wanted: City Manager (Applicants Apply Within)
I recall saying, as a city manager, both that I didn't get paid nearly enough and that I'd do the job for free. For every difficulty or impossible challenge, there is also a deep feeling of honor and of being an important part of something bigger than yourself. Like they say in the Peace Corps, it's "the toughest job you'll ever love."

Acknowledgments

I'm grateful to my publisher, Blue Light Press, for naming me a finalist in their 2025 Blue Light Book Award contest, especially Diane Frank for caring about this window into local government and allowing others to look through it as well.

I'm so thankful to Thomas Centolella, poet and educator, who helped me get the bureaucracy and "government speak" out of these poems, as much as I was able. My College of Marin classmates also made the poems better and always encouraged and supported me, particularly Tyra Ferlatte who copy edited this book. I'm indebted also to poet Kathy Evans who gave me insightful feedback on my poems, loaned me books of poetry greats, and made many great cups of tea.

Huge thanks to Kate Colin and Kip Harkness for being among the first readers of my collection and saying such nice things about it on my back cover! Also thank you to my friends Kelly Kline, Danielle and Sean O'Leary, Nadine Atieh Hade, Matthew Hymel, and Michael Ashley who read very early, messy versions of these poems, offered keen insight and perspective, and still kept me as a friend.

So much gratitude to all the elected officials and staff that I worked with in my 30+ years in local government. These poems are a tribute to you. All the love to my department director team at the City of San Rafael. Thank you for always "being togethery" and for being the best team I've ever been on. All of you show up in these poems in so many ways.

So much appreciation and love to my parents, my sister,

and all of my family and in-laws. My children, Griff Ballard and Lindy Ballard, served as editors, thought partners, chief supporters, and they designed the cover with me.

Thank you to the Douglas firs and coast redwoods of the Pt. Reyes National Seashore, where the first drafts of all of these poems were dictated into my phone.

Lastly, endless gratitude to my wife, Hannah Ballard. As I said to her — this book is not dedicated to you because my entire life is dedicated to you, so a book dedication seems kind of like small potatoes in comparison!

About the Author

Jim Schutz is a poet and former City Manager of San Rafael, California, with over 30 years of experience in local government that informs his distinctive voice and perspective. Jim brings rare authenticity to his poetry, exploring the unspoken challenges, quiet triumphs, and profound humanity of those who keep our cities running. He has published articles in professional journals on such topics as city management and leadership during difficult times.

www.ingramcontent.com/pod-product-compliance
Lightning Source LLC
Chambersburg PA
CBHW030908170426
43193CB00009BA/782